This is Brett.

Brett is my pet.

Brett does not like the vet.

"Go to the vet, Brett!"

The vet met my pet.

"No, Brett, no!"

"Let go of the vet."

"Let me get the net...

so I can get Brett."

"Get the pet in the net,"
said the vet.

"Not yet," said Brett.

Brett ran like a jet.

See the wet vet.

See the wet pet.

"What a mess, Brett!"

Yes, I like my pet.